Book Descripti

Toddlerhood is the stage o... ...e ones learn to crawl, wa... ...ate, and understand orders and reque... ...e more effective their communication and social skills, the better their chances of learning things quickly. Social skills allow children to have more meaningful and rewarding interactions. What they need from their parents is some encouragement and inspiration to allow healthy habits and skills to set in.

In this exceptionally-researched and relatable guide, parents can find answers to questions that have been bothering them for quite some time. How to raise sensible and compassionate toddlers? How to develop social skills? How to boost their self-esteem and self-worth? How to raise them to become independent and resilient? Luckily, Franks answers them all with the help of his seven proven strategies to build quality social skills, raise self-confidence, and promote accelerated learning so that children can have a promising future ahead.

Here's a sneak peek of what parents can expect to find inside:

- Why empathy makes learning social skills easier
- How teaching basic manners can be life-changing for tots

professional advice. The content within this book has been derived from various sources. Please consult a licensed professional before attempting any techniques outlined in this book.

By reading this document, the reader agrees that under no circumstances is the author responsible for any losses, direct or indirect, that are incurred as a result of the use of the information contained within this document, including, but not limited to, errors, omissions, or inaccuracies.

Before we begin, I have something special waiting for you. An action-packed 1 page printout with a few quick & easy tips taken from this book that you can start using today to become a better parent right now!

It's my gift to you, free of cost. Think of it as my way of saying thank you to you for purchasing this book.

Claim your download of Profoundly Positive Parenting with Frank Dixon by scanning the QR code below and join my mailing list.

Sign up below to grab your free copy, print it out and hang it on the fridge!

Sign Up By Scanning The QR Code With Your Phone's Camera To Be Redirected To A Page To Enter Your Email And Receive INSTANT Access To Your Download

Before we jump in, I'd like to express my gratitude. I know this mustn't be the first book you came across and yet you still decided to give it a read. There are numerous courses and guides you could have picked instead that promise to make you an ideal and well-rounded parent while raising your children to be the best they can be.

But for some reason, mine stood out from the rest and this makes me the happiest person on the planet right now. If you stick with it, I promise this will be a worthwhile read.

In the pages that follow, you're going to learn the best parenting skills so that your child can grow to become the best version of themselves and in doing so experience a meaningful understanding of what it means to be an effective parent.

Notable Quotes About Parenting

"Children Must Be Taught How To Think, Not What To Think."

— Margaret Mead

"It's easier to build strong children than to fix broken men [or women]."

- Frederick Douglass

"Truly great friends are hard to find, difficult to leave, and impossible to forget."

— George Randolf

"Nothing in life is to be feared, it is only to be understood. Now is the time to understand more, so that we may fear less."

— Scientist Marie Curie

Table of Contents

Introduction

Raising a toddler? What can be more fun than that?

Toddlerhood is a time of rapid development. It isn't just marked by the will to stand and walk but by much more that happens in their bodies and minds. It is a time for emotional, cognitive, and social development. Socialization and creating interactions are one of the many important aspects that mark these three to four years. Toddlers reach several milestones, and their ability to communicate and balance themselves on two feet are the two greatest and most pivotal ones to look for. With these in action, they are also introduced to several new emotions and feelings–many of which they don't comprehend yet.

As a parent, it is our ultimate goal to make things easier for our children. During toddlerhood, they are mostly dependent on us for all things from feeding to changing. They take up after our habits and mimic our style of walking, eating, sitting, or sleeping. They become inquisitive and want to poke their noses into things. They seek more freedom and independence.

We need to motivate social interactions from an early age. Toddlerhood seems to be the right age to start familiarizing yourself with the core concepts of the social skills you wish to develop in them. Social skills are a set of acceptable communication and interaction rules and strategies that help individuals form bonds with others and express themselves in both verbal and non-verbal ways. These include skills like communication, listening, coping, accountability, empathy, responsibility, and gratitude. These are the skills that allow humans, who are social creatures, to interact with one another without breaching the rules that make conversations uncomfortable.

The advantages of teaching good social and emotional skills to children go beyond the eloquent relationships that they will have with peers and relatives. Children with robust social skills experience less stress later in their lives, as per some ground-breaking studies. The earliest noticeable change, according to one study, was their reduced stress in daycare settings (Segrin & Flora, 2000). Where other kids cried and screamed, children with good social skills and empathy showed discipline and eagerness to help and be included.

Excellent social skills have also been linked to better performance in academics and a brighter future. According to a study published in the American Journal of Public Health in collaboration with the Penn State and Duke University, children that are emotionally and socially confident and disciplined in kindergarten have a better chance of succeeding in adulthood (Jones et al., 2015). It proposed a strong link between children with good social skills and college. It was revealed that children who knew more about sharing, cooperative, collaboration, and listening at the age of five had a better chance of going to college. They were also expected to have a full-time job at the age of 25.

Good social skills also help children pick things up faster. Since they are growing at a fast pace, you may be astonished to see how much they change every day in terms of their habits, speech, memory, and personality. The brain expands during the first two years which means that they are all set to take in more information, retain it, and process it. This is one reason why many parents stress teaching their children a foreign language as there is a much better chance that they will learn to speak and understand it at this age. Another reason to get started with social skills development early on is that this is also the time to promote accelerated learning. The more socially comfortable they are, the more expressive and open they will be. The more in control they feel about their actions and words, the more knowledge they will be able to pick up. This results in learning about new things easily and at a faster pace.

For instance, if we look at children, they don't usually have a sense of personal space. Teaching them how to communicate while respecting personal space, views, and boundaries makes them a more desirable candidate to form a bond with. On the other hand, children who don't know how to communicate or respect one another's uniqueness often have a difficult time making friends or finding people that stick with them through thick and thin.

Keeping all these crucial points in mind, we can't undermine the importance of good social skills. Therefore, in this book we shall talk about how parents can get started with teaching their toddlers how to develop excellent social skills using seven effective and proven strategies. We shall look at each in detail, determine how it helps children become more resourceful, and learn of several ways in which parents can implement those strategies to raise kids with exceptional social skills that promote accelerated learning.

Chapter 1: Understanding Social Skill Development in Toddlers

Toddlers are called toddlers because they are in that stage of development where they can't fully walk straight or are just learning to. It is derived from the word toddle which means to do the same. Toddlerhood begins when the child reaches the one-year mark. Scholars can disagree on when it ends as some suggest the developmental period ends when the child turns three, while others argue that it ends when the child reaches the four-year mark. Ideally, it ends when the child starts preschool, which isn't the same for every child. In some countries, children start school as early as three whereas in others, they don't go to school before the age of five, like in most states in the U.S.

From infancy, babies learn to form relationships with the people around them. They may not be the best judge of characters or features for that matter, but they do have strong hearing and smell senses. They can easily distinguish their mother's voice and smell when they are in their arms. Although crying is the only form of communication they know, they only nurture their skills as they grow older. As they reach toddlerhood, they are more expressive, understand several emotions like happiness, pain or sadness, and recognize people better. This makes interactions more meaningful. In this first chapter, we shall look at the various socio-emotional developmental milestones toddlers achieve to gain valuable insight into how they form relationships and learn about discipline. This will hopefully enable parents to devise the right strategies that work best in developing their social skills as well as promote accelerated learning. However, before we begin, keep in mind that each child is unique in their own way. Some are quick to pick things up while others are slow learners. This means that not every child will start to talk and walk right after they turn one. Some may be more expressive or active than others. If that is the case, there isn't a need to panic, as every child learns things at their own pace.

Socio-Emotional Developmental Milestones at Age One

Most of the social cues toddlers pick up are from their parents, especially mothers. It is the "the monkey see, monkey do" stage where they don't understand the reasoning behind a behavior but still do it.

You can expect them to point and express their intentions in whatever vocabulary they have learned in the past year. You can do the same. To promote accelerated learning, point towards things you want them to know about or remember. Keep in mind that it is less likely that they will remember it as their memory isn't equipped to do that just yet.

They are also able to recognize familiar faces like that of their parents, grandparents, siblings, babysitter, or doctor. They will start greeting them with a smile or a 'hi' and will willingly interact with them without supervision. By this age, they should be able to pay attention to the people around them and memorize their faces and voice. If they don't, this could be a red flag you need to talk about with your child's doctor.

They should also be able to engage with you on a one-on-one basis such as hand you things or take them from you. This again shows their eagerness to interact with you. They should also pick up the concept of taking turns, but this isn't a compulsion. Most kids have a tough time sharing their stuff with others.

They should also seek some independence whether they have started to walk or not. They will want to explore things and move towards them to give their curious mind some explanation.

Socio-Emotional Developmental Milestones at Age Two

By the time your child turns two, they should be able to better assess the things around them and become more engaged and inquisitive. They should be able to start parallel play by two. Parallel play refers to a child playing alongside another child but not together. They may occasionally exchange or share things together but don't expect too much too early.

They still need to learn to wait for their turn and share their toys or food with others. If they are already doing so, go ahead and praise their effort. Otherwise, they are ready to defend their toys the minute someone tries to touch them. Their social behavior stems from egotism because they have egocentric thinking. Their behaviors are directed by their desires.

Moreover, this is the age when children start to engage with strangers with some confidence. They will wave at the cashier or smile at a passerby. Their reaction or response is a sign that they want to explore more and interact more. Not every child is this open and expressive about their desires which means if yours is, you need to encourage that. Inquisitiveness is a sign of intelligence. The more curious the child about the things around them, the more information they will take in about things.

Socio-Emotional Developmental Milestones at Age Three

By the time they turn three, you might be starting to think about putting them into preschool. They are more talkative than ever before. They are full of energy and the stability in their walking gives them more confidence to seek independence. Their social skills start to develop too as they interact with others more and more. They may even have a few friends they like to play with or share their toys with. It could be a sibling, a parent, or a child of their age.

This is the age when children start to engage in associative play. This means that they actively seek someone to play with them. Their attention span also increases and they are more motivated to pretend play. This is the right time when you, as their parent, have to provide them with ample opportunities to increase positive interactions so that they don't feel shy around strangers. This will give you and your child a less traumatizing time when they start preschool as they will feel comfortable around others.

They will develop a basic understanding regarding safety rules such as why they shouldn't play with the knife, why they shouldn't tease the pet, or why they must stay away from the stairs altogether.

They will also start to listen better which means you can start requesting and ordering things from them. These can come in the form of gentle reminders that don't seem like an order but rather a request.

They should also have a better grasp of emotions by age three. They may experience sadness or anger firsthand. This is the time when you need to encourage good social behaviors and how to deal with them without crying, whining, or throwing things. During such social complications, try to make them feel better by hugging or kissing them to show empathy.

Finally, their imagination will improve. They will start pretend-play. They will concoct scenarios in their head. If they are into cars, they may come up with a scenario like a traffic situation or a train that has gone over the rail, and an ambulance and fire-truck is headed to help them. When they reach this stage, start reading stories to them about the things in which they show interest. If they are into wildlife animals, read them stories about the animals helping each other out, obeying their parents, or portraying good basic manners. Stories are a great way to get your word across.

Now that we know of what to expect in terms of their social and emotional development, we can use strategies and parenting tips that seem appropriate for their certain age. In the following chapters, we shall discuss how parents can prepare themselves with the right tools and measures to develop excellent social skills that aid them when starting preschool.

Chapter 2: The Seven Proven Strategies for Toddlers to Develop Social Skills

Every child has a way of looking at the world. They have different styles approaching people and things. Some are shy and introverted while others just jump and leap for everything. Some have a hard time leaving their parent's side while others are running away from them. This is what we call a child's temperament. Your child's temperament may differ from their friend or your sister's child. Your toddler may take longer to warm up to others and prefer assessing situations from a distance rather than jumping into them. Temperament is an individualistic characteristic that makes parenting harder. There is no one-size-fits-all here or a GPS that voices in which direction you need to steer.

Many people are quick to judge other parenting styles. They think they have it all figured out and give their suggestions inconsiderably. They think that we aren't doing enough and therefore have children who behave poorly and are ill-mannered. This isn't always the case. Sometimes, despite trying, some kids just don't listen or obey commands. This is where knowing their temperament comes into play. You need to know what works for them and what doesn't. You need to find things that interest them enough to take action. You need to find their strengths and weaknesses to support their unique needs.

Connecting with them is the first step towards teaching any type of skill or habit. They need to look at you as an authority figure as well as a friend. They need to see you as their role model and idol, and this can only happen if they trust you and your judgment.

If you are responsive to their needs, they will stay attuned to yours. If they see you practicing good social skills and manners, they will learn the same. To teach good social skills and use them to improve accelerated learning will take time. Toddlers have poor attention spans and everything around them is more interesting than what you want them to focus on. Teaching effective social skills is an art and no parent has won the medal for it so far. There are, of course, millions of parents but everyone has a different reward in mind. Some want to teach their kids social skills because they want them to prosper in their careers, some want them to have deep and meaningful relationships, while some want them to build self-confidence and self-worth.

Whichever goal you are after, one thing is for certain: You want them to be the happiest child in the world. You want them to have the best of everything. You want to protect them from harm's way and ensure that they remain cared for and looked after.

We want to begin developing excellent social skills in them and improve their chances at accelerated learning. Below are seven effective strategies that will help teach them about manners, obedience, discipline, coping skills, communication, listening skills, and stress management as they grow older and enter into their teens.

Empathize

Empathy allows you to be closer to your toddler and understand them better. If you want them to obey you and be respectful, you ought to do the same. It is one of the most effective ways to get to know your child better. Sympathize with them and let them know that you understand what they are going through. Being empathetic offers parents a great opportunity to build strong relationships with their children. When the connection is strong, they will most likely do all that you want them to do out of love and mutual respect.

Teach Basic Manners

Basic manners and etiquette come well before social skills. Think of it as the first step of the ladder. With good manners, children have an easier time connecting with others, making new friends, and forming bonds. It makes them preferred playmates and it makes them disciplined.

Promote Parallel Play

Your child may not be into other kids and will prefer to play on their own, even when in a room full of kids. Firstly, there is no harm in that as it is the first step towards learning about collaboration and social play. Encouraging them will only make transitioning from parallel play to social play smoother and faster.

Encourage Expression

Expression or communication is one of the areas that they need to work on the most since they are only starting to build their vocabulary. The more responsive and talkative they are, the quicker they will learn things. Encouraging expression is also essential to build resilience and regulate negative emotions using healthy coping mechanisms.

Praise

Praise and appreciation is also essential to improve behavior and instill positive habits in children–especially in toddlers who have a mind of their own. Praise and appreciation can fuel them with the right motivation and support to fulfill their dreams and aspirations. It will also make it easier for you to communicate with them in a positive manner and help develop good social skills.

Fuel Passions

Being supportive of their passions and dreams allows parents to be an active participant in their lives. One of the most common complaints of parents is that their toddler doesn't listen to them. To eliminate misbehavior and to help them develop healthy social skills, one needs to spend time with them communicating. Showing support for their passions can be a great conversation starter and it can make you their go-to person to talk to. While they talk to you, you can continue to teach them about good social skills and their importance.

Role-Play Scenarios

Finally, role-playing scenarios with your toddler allows them to make sense of the feelings of others. It gives them a different perspective to look at life and helps them feel the impact of their actions and behaviors. It is a great way to teach empathy as well as build social skills, which ultimately helps parents raise confident, self-reliant, and resilient individuals.

Chapter 3: Empathize, Empathize, Empathize

Empathy is the art of viewing the world from another's eyes. Empathetic people can understand what another person feels in a given moment and realize why someone else's actions in a particular situation make sense. Empathy allows us to understand the point of view of others when they wish to communicate their ideas and thoughts with us. It improves social interactions and it can be referred to as one of the most pivotal foundational blocks of social skills.

Since humans thrive on social connections, we all must learn about empathy and practice it in our daily lives. We are all born with seeds of concern and worry for others. Take the relationship between a mother and a child or a brother and a sister. We all hold compassion for one another and want to see each other succeed in life. As we grow older and we form more connections with others, we become less concerned about the immediate relationships we have. We forget about the love and attention our parents gave us when we were younger. We neglect their personal feelings and emotions and rarely have time to sit beside them and ask them how they feel. But, since we know that good social interactions rely on understanding one another, we need to take into account the fact that everyone wants to be heard. If we have a problem, do we not want to share it with someone and hope that they will understand? Similarly, others want the same care and attention that is genuine and is pure from all forms of judgment.

How do you nurture that? How do you become empathetic yourself and hopefully raise children who are empathetic too?

First of all, we are designed to empathize with others naturally. Our brains are wired in a way that we can feel the emotions that someone else is feeling. Have you ever seen a video where someone scares somebody during a prank? Do you not scream with them? Or perhaps you saw someone hit their hand with a hammer. Did you not wince? This is proof that humans are capable of empathizing with others.

For kids in their toddlerhood, their lack of communication skills often becomes a roadblock. They are unable to express themselves as they lack the right vocabulary for it. However, that doesn't mean that they don't experience any big feelings. If we think about it, it can all be rather confusing for them. This is where empathy comes in. They want to feel heard and validated and with empathy, you can do so. You can make them understand that you understand their state of despair and what they are going through.

How Toddlers Can Benefit From Empathy

Let's imagine for a minute a world without empathy. Everyone is mean and self-centered. No one cares about the opinions of others and everyone gets offended the second someone comes up with a conflicting viewpoint. Does it not seem like a toxic environment for a child to grow up in? Would you want your child to have the same self-centered and privileged beliefs?

As we get more innovative with technology and get artificial intelligence (AI) to replace most human jobs, employers start valuing only those who encompass a complex and varied set of skills. Today's world is a world of collaboration. Take conglomerates as an example. They have several products and services that fall into different niches. They need people who can collaborate, think effectively, and find solutions to unique problems with a unique and effective approach. The more minds working together, the greater the chance of a conflict. How well will your child do in such a competitive and collaborative environment if they are unable to hear what others have to say?

Numerous studies suggest a strong correlation between socio-emotional skills and a child's learning ability. We believe that if our child does well in studies, they must have good social and emotional skills too. Wrong. Research shows that achievements and cognitive development only guarantee 50% success at school. The remaining 50% is guaranteed by how socially and emotionally developed the child is.

Other than that, empathy also nurtures the conditions essential for creativity. Creativity can strike at any minute. It can find us in the shower or during a traffic jam. It can't be summoned on command as it flourishes under openness, understanding, and acceptance. Being able to open oneself to the views of others takes courage as it accounts for trying something new. It also opens doors to being creative. When a toddler understands others and is accepting of their presence, it means that they are open to the possibility of taking risks and trying new things. An example of this would be going to new and unfamiliar places or meeting new people. If they don't cry, whine, or scream when someone touches them and they are inviting with big smiles on their faces, they are accepting of the newness and uncertainty.

Empathy also encourages logical thought processes and rational patterns. Many neuroscientists believe that when children come from a place of empathy, they are better equipped to cope with the daily stresses and challenges of life with reason, clarity, and purpose. They feel more competent to regulate their emotions and respond better.

Another benefit is less aggression in children. Toddlerhood is the age where children start to build vocabulary and of all the words they love the most, 'no' becomes their favorite. They respond to most things with 'no.' Additionally, when they can express themselves better and get their way, their demands increase too. When these demands remain unmet, children become angry and frustrated. However, if a child is empathetic, they might be able to see the reasoning and logic behind the rejection. Their reactions become less destructive and out of control. They will stop acting out and behave with calmness instead.

There is also evidence that children who lack empathy turn out to be selfish, boorish, and narcissistic. They are more likely to bully others and they have difficulty staying in a group. They are self-centered individuals who don't have compassion towards others. If this doesn't change, they may have a hard time making friends or finding the right partner for themselves. They can also have a troubled time being part of a community and they might remain alienated from everyone. They need to become tolerant of others. They need to learn compassion. Luckily, empathy teaches them to become compassionate and selfless.

Learning to Be Empathetic - Getting Started

We now know how critical empathy is for children and the role it plays in shaping their personality. It is best to start as early as possible. As parents, the first thing you need to do is model empathy in your words and actions. Toddlers imitate the things they see. Even when they don't know the reasoning behind their actions, they mimic the actions of their parents. Teaching them about empathy will help them build good social skills and improve their interactions and bonds with potential friends and partners in the future. Here are some strategies for you to introduce the concept of empathy and model it yourself.

Use Play Cards

Use flashcards or books to depict various emotions and situations where the protagonist shows empathy towards the victim. Reading to your child about empathy using stories is a much better way to interact and get your word across. The more interactive and engaging the stories or cards, the bigger the possibility that they will pick the habit up.

Encourage Problem-Solving

Instead of coming up with a solution when your child is faced with a troubling situation or challenge, let them find one on their own. For instance, let's say their sibling has snatched a toy from their hand. What will they do? Do they cry right away and look for some help from you or do they let their sibling play with it for some time because they think the sibling needs it too? Their reaction will tell you two things. First, it will tell you how empathetic or non-empathetic they are in general, and second, it will let you know how much work needs to be done with them. When toddlers are allowed to do what seems fitting to them, it also builds their confidence and improves self-worth.

Reason Using Examples

Label the feelings or emotions that they are experiencing and try to normalize them. Secondly, show vulnerability in front of them so they know that others feel emotions too. Give them reasons compelling enough to understand and comply with. For instance, if you are afraid they will fall down the stairs, let them know your fears. Let them know how much it will hurt them and hurt you if they fall down the stairs and get injured. When toddlers think that the reasons make sense, they are more likely to abide by the rules set in place.

Show Moral and Ethical Support

If you ever find your child struggling with a difficult emotion such as sadness or pain, let them know that you understand their feelings and appreciate them for having the courage to go through it. Your support, even just verbal, will have a deep impact on them. They will feel a lot better if they know someone understands their situation. Use such instances to teach the importance of strong coping skills and show them how they can deal with big feelings in healthy ways. For example, if your child's trip to the zoo was canceled last minute, say something like, "I know you wanted to go to the zoo badly. I know you must be angry that we didn't get to go this weekend. How about we go next week and later go for ice cream too?"

Chapter 4: Teach Basic Manners

Toddlers aren't old enough to distinguish between right and wrong. They will, however, do as directed. For example, they may not understand why they shouldn't hit others or maintain a safe distance from them but if they are directed to do so, they will. Why? It's because their parents told them to and also because they will be punished if they don't. They simply know that they must obey elders and respect others but without the literal reasoning.

This is where teaching them about basic manners comes in. They may not know why they need to say thank you but they will learn to say it if they are taught the right way. Teaching basic skills teaches them about courtesy, which is again important if they wish to have fruitful and happy interactions with others. Toddlers having difficulty controlling their impulses can be taught to use words like excuse me, sorry, and thank you to appear well-mannered. Being mannerly is a social skill that parents must develop in their children. It is important because it will allow them to get along with others in a kind and friendly way. Take an ill-mannered kid for example. Suppose you set up a playdate with an ill-mannered kid and your child. From the minute the two start to interact, the ill-mannered child pulls on your child's hair, hits him, snatches things from his hands, and makes your child feel miserable. Would you let that kid near your child again? Mannerly kids make preferred playmates. They get invited for playdates more than those who aren't mannerly. If your child is obedient and courteous, he already has a better chance to interact and make new friends.

Secondly, being courteous also demonstrates respect. Saying thank you upon receiving something or saying sorry for mistakenly hurting somebody shows that you come from a good and respectable family.

Toddlers who are taught manners early also build integrity. They become likable and desirable to be around. On the other hand, children who lack basic manners aren't the most pleasing to be around. They have a tough time at school and daycare because they can't get along with the rest of the kids and they feel alienated. No one wants to play with them and this only makes them act out more.

As a parent, it should be your goal to teach your child about basic manners as early as possible. Habits take time to set in. It is much easier to train a younger and eager mind than to train a developed and mature mind.

The Important Role Learning Good Manners Plays

Good manners allow young kids to convey respect. When one hears words like thank you from someone, they feel appreciated. When one hears sorry from someone, it removes the feeling of being wronged. When someone says excuse me, it shows respect for the person's right to not do something that has been asked. These are all signs of good character traits that teach one about respect for others and show appreciation for them.

If you teach your child these basic manners when they are young, you are doing them a big favor. From potential employers to partners, their ethics and morals will set the stage for them. Picture this: Your son goes for his first interview. He qualifies for the job in terms of his skills and qualification but lacks basic manners. Therefore, as he enters the room, he doesn't knock before entering, and when he moves towards the chair, he doesn't ask if he has the permission to sit. He interrupts the employer repeatedly, acts rude, and doesn't show respect towards an elderly manager. Do you think that company will see him as the right candidate? Do you think he will get the job? Let's not get ahead this far. Let's imagine a scenario where your child goes to the park. He doesn't let other kids have a turn on the swings, he pushes them around deliberately, and he complains back when confronted. What will the other parents think about you and your child? Do you think they will respect you or your child? Good manners go a long way when it comes to developing social skills in kids. It is the key to making interactions more conducive and pleasant.

How to Emphasize Teaching Manners

Toddlerhood itself has several stages. It expands over three years, each year with its unique features. Each stage promotes physical, emotional, and mental abilities. Behaviors differ in different stages of growth. As parents, we need to recognize which behaviors are expected at each age. For instance, if a child has just turned one, their communication skills will be different than when they turn three or four. But as always, starting early gives you an edge in shaping behavior and temperament. To build a solid foundation in social skills, you must approach them with the following strategies in mind.

Turn Dinner Times Into Conversation Times

Dinner time is a great opportunity to talk about the day's activities and highlights. If both parents work, you can ask the child about their day at the daycare. You can ask them if they made any new friends today, heard a new story, or learned a new poem. Dinner times offer an excellent chance to encourage communication and practice basic manners. You can teach them how they should eat, how to say thanks, and how to have normal conversations where one waits for their turn to speak and doesn't interrupt in between. You can also teach table manners, why they should respect the food they consume, and why they shouldn't waste things.

Reward Them When They Do Something Good

If you catch your toddler saying "thank you" or 'sorry,' never let it pass without appreciation or some form of reward. We are all motivated and driven by rewards. Be it a promotion at work or a sales coupon in a fashion magazine, we all love to be rewarded or appreciated. To emphasize and encourage the habit of good manners, never leave an opportunity to appreciate them when they depict good manners. Soon they will start to associate good manners with reward and be more motivated to use them.

Make It a Habit

Whenever your child receives something from someone, remind them to say thank you first and then hand it to them. The same goes for saying 'please' when they want something from someone. This promotes respect for others as well as increases the value of the things received. Teaching them to say thank you whenever someone gives them something will develop into a habit in no time.

Emphasize Graciousness

When competing, you don't always win. Sometimes you lose and it can be heartbreaking. You feel humiliated, mocked, and like the weaker person. No one likes to feel that and certainly not your little one. They may start to cry, scream, hit the other child, or act out by throwing things in aggression. This happens when they are unable to digest the loss.

Teach them healthy ways to accept defeat. Moreover, teach them not to gloat when they win or make the other person feel like the loser. Teach graciousness. Good sportsmanship is a must whether you win or lose. It must be taught to children early on as it prevents cases of jealousy, envy, and anger later in life.

Teach Good Playdate Manners

If you have been invited to a playdate with your toddler or have welcomed guests at your home, teach your child about how to make the other child feel welcome. Remind them of the rules like greeting, sharing, and waiting for their turn in a relaxed manner. Also, tell them to always clean up after they are done playing whether at their home or someone else's. If you are taking them to someone's house, sit them down and talk to them about not placing their feet on the furniture, running in the house, or touching things without permission. If you are the one hosting, tell them to let the guests eat first, be courteous, share their toys, and put the toys they don't want to share away before the friend comes over. This will prevent most of the snatching, hitting, or pulling.

Talk to Them About the Importance of Waiting

Kids this age can be restless. It can be hard to make them sit in one place. When they speak, they want to say as much as they can in a second. Teach them to calm down when expressing themselves so that they can be understood. Additionally, teach them about how important it is to hear others and to wait for their turn to speak. Model this by speaking calmly at all times and being genuinely interested in what they have to say. Also, don't encourage the habit of interrupting others and make it a point to let others complete their sentence first. Good listening and communicating skills are an essential part of developing good social skills. Be sure to make a note of it.

Chapter 5: Introduce Parallel Play

Imagine this: You organized a playdate for your tot. You invited a few kids along with their parents. You laid out your child's many toys and told the parents to bring their child's favorite ones too. After an hour of play, you notice an odd thing. Your child is playing and so are the other kids. But they aren't playing together but rather alongside each other. What's up with them? Why aren't they socializing? At this age and stage, it should happen naturally, right?

Yes, but here's the thing. Unlike other skills, children don't learn social skills from their peers. Instead, they learn them from you. Your toddler is still young and prefers to play with familiar faces. Let's call that their inner circle. Even when positioned in a room full of toys and a few other kids, they would still prefer to play alone than with those kids. This happens because they haven't yet developed the social and emotional skills they need to interact with others.

Parallel play can be interpreted as a small phase in the life of a toddler where they choose to play alongside other children as opposed to with them. Interaction between the kids is nearly zero with an occasional smile, tug, or pulling incident between them. This is the first step to learning to play collaboratively and it sets the stage for shared play. As weird as it sounds, this is a normal phase. This should be encouraged, says Dr. Dana Cohen, a child psychologist at the Beaumont Children's in Royal Oak who specializes in children with autism and other special needs.

Why Parallel Play?

Ideally, parallel plays look exactly like it sounds. Two children play in close proximities, focused on their separate toys and games. Dr. Dana believes that children who don't engage in parallel play during their early years and prefer to remain isolated or are shy in the presence of another child may be showing signs of autism. There are many benefits to parallel play. For instance, it develops a child's motor skills. When a toddler engages in parallel play, they only focus on the resources they have in a controlled environment. They notice the behavior and actions of the other child and begin to imitate them. Their responses become coordinated. They learn to observe and modify. This is a great skill to foster in children as it shows that they can focus and follow. If they are to learn some sport or game, they will observe and learn to imitate actions by observing actual players. Suppose they are playing catch with you, they will soon learn to pick up the way you throw the ball at them and even pick up something entirely new.

Secondly, it helps in the development of communication skills. When children are left to play with themselves alongside other kids, they also pick up the words and language they use. They eventually start to talk to one another too. If they are at the park and someone yells to catch the ball, they will look at the child first and then at the ball and learn new words in the process.

Encouraging Parallel Play

How do you begin encouraging your child to parallel play? For starters, parallel play should occur in a safe and homely environment. This means that it has to take place in a place that isn't too crowded like the park or daycare, and second, it should occur in the presence of at least one parent of each child so that the children don't feel anxious around strangers. Keep in mind that the goal is to let them transition from this phase to the phase where they willingly start to interact with one another without being forced to. Keep the duration of the social play restricted but not too short. Give the child an ample amount of time to get accustomed to the surroundings and see if they seem interested in the other child or not. At first, the child will feel some stress and thus may not take part in any sort of play out of fear. Giving them some time to relieve their stress will prepare them to be more engaging next time.

Don't Force Them

When encouraging parallel play, let the toddler embrace momentary independence. If they don't seem interested in the play and would rather be roaming around the room, don't force them to sit down and play with the toys in front of them. Enforcement won't get you the desired results. Instead, it will only make the child act out and experience stress.

Have Enough Toys

Ensure that both the children have enough toys to play with. This means bringing out all the bricks, blocks, dolls, cars, stuffed animals, play dough, coloring books, and toy sets. A great tip is to have more toys that promote cognitive thinking and problem-solving so that you can kill two birds with one stone. No child should be made to feel left out with fewer toys. If you are determined to initiate social play early on, put all of the toys in the center of the room and let them choose their favorites themselves. However, keep an eye out for any fights, pulling, or pushing.

Keep Distractions to a Minimum

Limit the number of distractions in the room the kids are in. The more distractions there are, the less interested they will be in the actual play. If they aren't too clingy, you and the other parent can let them play on their own in a separate room and keep checking in on them every five to 10 minutes. Remember, the goal is to build social skills and encourage social interactions. This is only possible when they are by themselves in the room. Also, if possible, reduce the number of toys after each playdate so that children feel more encouraged to interact with the limited availability of toys in front of them.

Know When to Upgrade

Finally, notice the behavior and actions of your child at every playdate. This will help you know when they are ready for the transition to collaborative play or play with another friend instead of alone. When you feel they are ready, subtly nurture direct interactions by making them sit together and share toy sets, puzzles, or coloring books. Encourage them to take turns playing and sharing their toys.

Chapter 6: Encourage Expression

With a limited vocabulary, toddlers aren't the greatest communicators. They need to learn to be able to express themselves better. Encouraging expression and seeking their opinion on little matters can help establish a trusted relationship and encourage toddlers to be more open about their problems and needs.

The more expressive they are about their wants and needs, the easier it will be to develop social skills since you will know exactly which areas they lack in. For instance, if you notice that your toddler loves to speak but is a poor listener, you can always encourage listening activities to teach them about the importance of listening and enhance that social skill.

All great ideas are born in the mind. However, they can die a terrible death if no one ever hears of them. The ability to express oneself effectively is an art. Children are natural storytellers. They are creative and imaginative. Nothing is impossible in their eyes. The better they are at expressing themselves, the better their quality of life and future prospects. The ability to communicate effectively is a key skill, and the better we are at it, the better our quality of life will be.

Humans have been communicating from the minute they were born. The first cry of a baby is a way to let the parents know they have arrived. As they grow from a baby to toddler, it becomes a parent's job to nurture good communication skills which will help them express themselves better and learn things at a quicker pace. When children feel confident in expressing themselves, their self-esteem also improves.

If we look at a child's developmental stages, we notice that they first start to communicate with their parents, then with their siblings, and then with their peers and educators. All that they learn, they learn from us–the parents. Thus, the more expressive, descriptive, and comfortable we are with our words and actions, the more comfortable they will be too.

Good Communication Skills and Social Skills Development

Communication is a fundamental developmental milestone in a toddler's life. We all want to be heard and be understood. Being able to express ourselves allows us to form relationships and improve social interactions. For a child, they need to express themselves in the same manner too. They use limited vocabulary and actions to express themselves. However, if we allow them to be more expressive by teaching them the right ways to say and do things, we can improve conversations and enhance the stability of parent-child relationships.

Communication also develops a special bond with the caregiver. The more time they spend together communicating, the stronger the bond gets. It leads to close connection with one or more of the immediate family members which becomes important as the child grows into a teenager and starts to keep things private and secret.

Having a vocabulary at an early age and knowing how to use it also helps the child learn things easily during school. It increases the likelihood that your child will pick things up faster than the other kids since they will already have an improved vocabulary by the time they start preschool. They will be quicker at taking instructions from their educators which will make learning easier and more interesting for them.

It must also be noted that children who aren't good at expressing themselves or have poor speech abilities have a difficult time with reading, spelling, and oral exercises. The parents have to work harder to improve the learning ability of the child. Besides, when they are unable to express themselves, frustration also sets in. You must know this if you have ever played charades with a partner that doesn't take the cues well. A minute into the game and you already feel frustrated for not being able to get your point across. The same is true with children. When they can't understand things clearly and they can't make others understand them, it becomes frustrating. The more they struggle, the more frustrated they get.

This is one reason why children with disabilities like autism or ADHD have a hard time with behavior modification. Children with diagnosed disorders can be hard to deal with for most parents and they will require assistance from schools that are designed particularly for their special-needs child.

Another aspect that often gets neglected is that when children don't know how to communicate, they have trouble making friends. Childhood friendships are especially important. When children suffer from poor self-esteem due to their poor communication skills, it can become a hindrance for them to get along with others. This can lead to increased anxiety and isolation which may become a mental health issue in the future.

Encouraging Openness

Your little one needs you and your support whether they can express themselves well or not. However, your job as a parent is to equip them with the right means to improve their communication skills as well as encourage expression. You need to get down on their level and make yourself approachable. You want them to see you as their supporter and mentor, not someone who will laugh at them for pronouncing something wrong or acting frustrated when they aren't able to convey their message. They should be able to see the willingness in you to understand them. Stay present and attentive to show your interest and concern for them. To improve any form of communication, both of the involved parties need to give their undivided attention. This is only possible when both are attentive to each other's needs and are active listeners. Some other great strategies to encourage the habit of expression so that children can learn great social skills include the following:

Read Stories

To improve vocabulary, foster the habit of reading in your children from an early age. Thanks to advancements in print media, you can always get your hands on interactive books. Some even come with sound effects to pique a child's interest. Make use of them and build the habit of reading with and to them. Stories are a great way to promote the expression of ideas, emotions, and thoughts. You can always ask questions about the characters or what they would do in a certain scenario.

Sing With Them

If they aren't into reading yet or are too young to understand, songs, rhymes, and poems can be your next best weapon. Poems and songs with simple and easy-to-recall lyrics can be a great way to build vocabulary and teach emotions. For example, if the poem is about a kid that has lost his bat, you can use it to teach sadness and happiness and how one experiences those emotions. If there are any difficult or unfamiliar words in the song or the poem, you can help your child understand them.

Listen to Your Child

Let them have some time to respond when you ask them a question or are talking to them. When you are speaking to them, ensure that you maintain good eye contact. Be mindful of the words you use around them, even when you're talking to someone else. Although these tips seem small and insignificant, they can have a huge impact on the way a child communicates with others. Essentially, you have to teach them good listening skills because they won't be able to contribute a response if they aren't listening. Asking them questions and noticing how they are responding to them will tell you if they listened or not.

Narrate Your Daily Routines

Narrating things as you do them is another great way to encourage dialogue and openness. This will allow your child to create connections between your words and actions. For instance, if you are watering the flowers, you can say, "You are flowering the plants in the garden." If we take a look, there are at least three news words that they can learn: gardening, watering, and flowering. They might ask you about it themselves, or maybe they won't need to as soon as they see what you are doing. Keeping them in the loop in such a manner will help them build vocabulary and become more curious about things around the house. Curious kids are often intelligent and fast learners.

Make Requests Clear

When teaching about openness and good communication skills, don't forget to set clear and realistic expectations. Every child has unique skills. They take their own good time to learn things. Just because a colleague's son is saying full sentences by age three doesn't mean your child should too. Sure, you can try a little harder with them but don't expect them to comply with the standards. They are too young to be thrown into a competition of "who does it better." They are kids, full of life and energy, let them be that! When making requests or giving instructions, be as clear as possible and ensure that they have understood what is expected of them.

Don't Correct Them

Sometimes, your child is going to pronounce words wrong. Instead of mocking or correcting them, simply repeat the right pronunciation of the word by using it in a sentence. This will prevent shattering their confidence and self-esteem. Keep in mind that the goal is to encourage openness rather than deter it. If you keep making fun of them, they might start to see you as a manipulator and stop coming to you with their ideas and problems altogether. Be subtle about the correction so that they don't feel judged.

Chapter 7: Praise Wholeheartedly

To encourage good social behaviors, children need motivation. Praise and appreciation go a long way. Why else would they sit quietly and act well-behaved when there is nothing motivating them? Praising good behaviors increases the likelihood of repetition.

Praise and appreciation lets your little one know that you like something about their behavior. It is about you being vocal about something they did positively. Praise nurtures a child's skills, boosting their self-esteem and confidence. They will be competent in the face of challenges. When we praise our children, we demonstrate how they can think and talk positively about others and themselves. It is a way to tell children how much we like a certain behavior of theirs. It's like a pat on the back!

In earlier times, praising a child was considered bad. It was believed that it resulted in boosting their ego in a bad way and that it made them think of themselves as superior. It made them overconfident and full of themselves. But times are now changing and as we gain more and more information about mental health issues in children and their lack of self-confidence, it seems selfish not to praise them. Today, with the help of many scientific brain studies, researchers strongly believe that praise and appreciation is a great way to reinforce positive behavior in children and build their social skills.

According to one study, the human mind responds to social approval in the same manner that it does to monetary rewards. This means that verbal praise and recognition has become as important as monetary rewards to encourage good behaviors. Besides, who doesn't like to be praised? It makes us all feel gooey and accomplished inside, even if just for a minute. The best part is, praise doesn't even have to be lengthy or descriptive. A simple, 'yay,' 'wow,' or applause is a great gesture to show appreciation.

Importance of Praise and Appreciation for Toddlers

Praise and appreciation is an excellent and effective way to encourage children to try again after they have failed (Morris and Zentall, 2014). Toddlers seek praise and encouragement from their elders. They are already in that phase of development where they rely on communication. They look up to them and wait for their approval over everything. It all seems exciting as they are developing new vocabulary every day. They feel especially motivated when they are praised over day-to-day tasks like finishing their vegetables, walking, or putting aside all their toys after playtime. Many parents attach a reward for good behavior to further elevate the feelings of happiness and accomplishment.

When children feel supported, their natural curiosity is encouraged. They feel more in control of their actions and they have a strong will to do things with perfection. They even start doing things they previously hated doing, just for the sake of some praise and appreciation.

Furthermore, toddlers that feel motivated by their parents or teachers also report better mental health and wellbeing. You don't need science to prove that kids who grow up in supportive households find it easier to follow their dreams and passions than those who don't feel encouraged.

Finally, when tots feel appreciated, they are more likely to repeat that behavior. Thus, if they have been up to some mischief lately or are giving you a tough time with their temper tantrums and disobedience, try praising them for the things they do well and notice how their behaviors will change drastically.

Learning to Appreciate - A Guide for Parents

How do you get started? Are there any rules about which behaviors get praise and which don't? What words do you use so that your child will know when they are being appreciated? First things first, make it a rule to point out more of the good in them than criticizing them over negative behaviors. Ideally, you should say at least six good things about your child before you say one bad, or negative, thing to them. They are at the age where good habits will find a home in their heart if they feel encouraged and motivated. Here is what you should appreciate.

Look for Small Successes

Praise shouldn't only be given over something major. Make it a habit to start praising your child for small and insignificant successes and accomplishments. Sometimes, we don't realize the amount of effort that has gone into something. Something that doesn't seem big to you might mean the world to them. Thus, don't hold back your praise and appreciation for big accomplishments only. Compliment them over little things too.

Reward Good Behavior

This isn't a requisite, but pairing your praise with something tangible (a reward) or intangible (a privilege) can also boost their confidence in their abilities and encourage the development of social skills and positive behaviors. Rewards add some oomph factor to a praise. They are the icing on the cake that can make all the difference.

Praise Efforts Too

Sometimes, your child will fail miserably. But that doesn't mean that they didn't make an effort. Praise shouldn't just follow an accomplishment. Effort should be praised too, equally. Doing so will motivate them to continue and not give up in themselves and their abilities. Let them know that you understand how hard they worked for something. They shouldn't have to feel like a failure.

Be Descriptive

Be clear and specific when praising them. If you want to encourage a particular behavior, they need to know that. Being descriptive allows you to hit the right mark. Being specific also makes the praise feel more wholesome and genuine. By doing so, you allow your child to know what behaviors and actions will earn them respect and appreciation from their parents, and they will hopefully try to be better at it too.

Chapter 8: Fuel Their Passions

Like praises, being supportive and encouraging towards a child's passions and dreams is another essential and proven strategy to develop productive social skills in kids.

There are several perks to showing interest and motivating your toddler to seek their passions and dreams. They may seem silly and short-term currently, but by showing support and interest you make them see how excited you are. It also makes their small missions seem bigger, challenging, and important. In the process, they pick up some great habits like the importance of staying true and focused on a task, demonstrating resilience, and going after their goals and dreams.

What is a passion, and is it the same as a dream or goal? According to Merriam-Webster, passion is a strong feeling of excitement and enthusiasm for something or someone. It isn't necessarily a trajectory for success. It doesn't guarantee that your child will get into the best schools and colleges or get a high-paid job. It is more about intrinsic happiness. It is a source of excitement for the one experiencing it, and it may or may not reap promising success. If a child is passionate about something, it doesn't mean that they will forever remain stuck to it. For example, they may enjoy learning about dinosaurs right now but that doesn't mean that they want to grow up to be a paleontologist. They may want to pursue an entirely different career and goal in their adult life. The thing about passion is that it can change as the kid grows up. In most cases, it does.

The Benefits of Supporting Your Child's Passions

The real question is why you should be supporting their passions? Well, here are some excellent reasons why.

For starters, pursuing one's passions releases the feel-good hormone called dopamine. When we force our toddlers into doing something, we take away the joy from it. Suddenly, it becomes a chore and not an interesting passion. Conversely, when they do something purely out of joy and because they want to, it makes them feel happy and more driven to bring it to completion. When children do things out of interest, their brains kick into the auto drive mode. It releases substantial amounts of dopamine which makes children feel the accomplishment they have achieved.

Secondly, when they are driven by passion they also feel more focused and determined. If they don't feel motivated, they may still complete the task but not with 100% dedication. If the task doesn't spark joy and they just do it for the sake of doing it, it won't boost their self-esteem.

Thirdly, when children are motivated to pursue their passions and aspirations, they are more likely to talk about them with others every chance they get. This will improve their social interactions, both by number and quality. Their pure interest in the subject will compel them to discuss it proudly with others and may very well become the hub of their social circle. Who knows, maybe they will find someone like-minded as themselves and become friends with them!

Finally, we also know that when kids work passionately towards achieving something, they are open to taking in as much information as they can regarding it. This means that their learning and general knowledge will also improve. Passion-based learning is deep-rooted in science. The more interested the child is, the higher the chances of them learning new things about it. They will show more interest in studying and gaining knowledge about the subject and they will develop a greater understanding for it.

Showing Support - The ABCs

As parents, it is our job to support and nurture our child's interests and passions. By doing so, we show them that we care about their interests and understand how important it is to them. This helps to create a compassionate bond between us and allows for more strong and open communication. To get started, here's how you can support their passions and show them that you care.

Know Their Interests

It may seem ritualistic to do the same things other parents do with their children when it comes to finding their interests and passions. Perhaps you think that they have a thing for sports because they are always sitting beside their dad watching the sports channel. You assume that sports must be their passion, but we urge you to dig in deeper. Don't assume things when it comes to your children. Maybe the sole reason they are watching sports is because they want to spend more time with their dad. Sports may or may not have anything to do with their interests. Thus, take the time to really get to know your child and notice what sparks their interests and lights up their eyes with anticipation. Observe them during playtime, ask questions to know them better, and be an active listener to know what subjects they are passionate about.

Follow Your Own Passion

Toddlers do as they see. If they see you skimping on your own passions, they will do the same–sooner or later. As parents, be a great role model to encourage the habit of following their passions religiously. It is important for them to see that you follow the advice you have for them and spend time doing the things that you love. Cultivating your passions will allow them to do the same and invest their time and energy into what they love.

Avoid Judging

Just because your child is madly into stamp collecting and is not interested in some sport that has a definite and promised future doesn't give you the right to belittle them. You may have had other plans for them but forcing them to try the things you want is no different than mentally imprisoning them. Many expecting parents have aspirations to see their kids take after their interests. Maybe you were really into baseball and hoped that one day your son will be too, but it doesn't necessarily mean that they will. Maybe their interests are different in nature. Maybe they hate all things sports. When this happens, resist the urge to criticize and pull their leg. Avoid judging them for having interests that don't fit your ideals. Encourage them through thick and thin and show support. Let them fulfil their desired needs without being too judgmental about them.

Chapter 9: Role-Play to Convey the Message

Sometimes toddlers need a taste of things to build good social skills and promote accelerated learning abilities, and to fully understand them. Your lecture may not hold any value unless they experience the thing they weren't supposed to do. If they hurt someone, they won't be able to feel the pain unless it happens to them too. How else will they be more compassionate and careful the next time?

Role-play is interpreted in different ways. Essentially, it is learning via play. Role-play is an extremely strong technique in developing social skills. It fuels the young mind with imagination and creativity. Using role-play as a teaching method during toddlerhood proves effective and beneficial. It helps our little ones create scenarios in their head and experience various emotions and feelings during play. Everyone can learn how to read, write, or do the math. But it takes real skill to imagine worlds that exist only in the mind and interact with others around them. Since social skills can only be learned naturally through observation and training, role-play serves as a useful tool to get started.

The Power of Role-Play

If you have ever been to a therapist or counselor in troubled times, do you recall how they used visualization and role-play frequently to play out scenarios in real life? Did you ever notice how often they used it to make us see the things we have been unable to see or experience before?

The benefits of role-playing in kids are varied. For starters, they enhance social and emotional skills in children. During role-play, kids place themselves in settings where they are required to interact with others to find solutions and answers to their problems. This also allows them to experience what empathy feels like and it allows them to depict it. It also builds resilience in children as they feel more confident at regulating their emotions, gaining control over them, and controlling their reactions to them.

As discussed before, role-play allows kids to expand their vision by imagination. It promotes creativity and enhances their skills and talents by developing a strong problem-solving approach.

Role-playing also enriches language and communication skills. Kids can pick up new words and experience different emotions. When they are exposed to different scenarios, their cognitive development improves and their vocabulary increases too. The more words they know, the more expressive they can be. The more expressive they are, the more confident they feel. They are in a better state to convey their message. This also comes in handy when they start to read and write.

Finally, we also see role-play as an effective method to teach kids about conflict resolution. When we encourage them to view the world from a different perspective, we prevent conflict of opinions as well as physical fights and arguments. Sometimes, they are unable to see the logical side of things because they feel overwhelmed by their emotions. Their actions and behaviors aren't a product of rational thinking. If this continues or is allowed to continue, kids will never learn to cope in healthy and meaningful ways. They will always see the world as they want to see it and thus have a hard time accepting others' opinions. They won't be able to work as part of a team and they will always feel more privileged than the rest of their peers.

Using Role-Playing Strategies to Instill Good Habits

Learning social skills using role-play sounds like a solid strategy for toddlers. They are always curious about stories and imaginative scenarios. They must have already started to pretend to play. Role-play is more effective than just sitting in a corner and playing with themselves. It requires interaction which can help toddlers in many ways. For starters, they can seek attention from you. Second, they can experience what it means to be in someone else's shoes, and third, it encourages them to modify their behaviors and actions. It is also more effective than any school lesson written down in a notebook for a test. Its unique feature; interaction leaves a lasting impression. Thus, if you are convinced that this can be a great start to teach toddlers about social skills and accelerated learning, we have plenty of ideas to help you.

Reverse the Roles

Taking turns can help children see different sides of things. If they have been hitting or pulling another child's hair, sit them down and talk to them about how the other child feels. Ask questions like, "How would you feel if I pulled your hair?" and "How would you feel if I snatched that toy from your hand right now?" Let them see how their actions affect others and how they would feel if the same were happening to them.

Make Them Watch a Movie

The best thing about movies and cartoons is that they depict a vast majority of emotions that children go through but are unable to cope with in better ways. Let your child watch a movie and whenever a character experiences an emotion, positive or negative, pause the movie to ask them how they would have felt at that moment. Ask them what they would have done to observe how developed their emotional skills are. Once the child has provided you with an answer, see if it needs to be altered. If it does, then this is a teaching moment you need to take advantage of. The character would have done something sensible too. Once you are done explaining your point of view, play the movie and together see how the character overcomes the challenge too.

Identify Emotions

Using the same strategy used above, you can also ask them to identify which emotion the character is going through and why. "I think he is angry because the rain hasn't stopped and he wanted to go play outside with his friends." Let them label the emotion and ask them why the character feels a certain way.

Organize a Tea Party

Get a bunch of their toy figures and ask your toddler to arrange for a tea party for them. Tell them that they will be the host of it and help them prepare for the party. Once the table has been set and all the figurines have been seated, pretend to serve tea and biscuits. Pretend to have a conversation about emotions, feelings, and the importance of etiquette. Use language like "Could you please pass me the sugar pot?" and when your child does, say thank you in return. Similarly, you can celebrate the birthday of a toy figure and have your child prepare a gift for the character. You can tell them what to say upon meeting them at the birthday party such as "Happy birthday! I have brought a gift for you; I hope you like it."

Encourage Reading Stories

Stories that explore emotions, basic manners, and end with good morals to teach are a great way to encourage good behavior. You can read the book in different voices to pique interest, and stimulate their creativity by asking them open-ended questions during the reading to see what they would have done in that situation.

Conclusion

Social skills are a set of essential skills for children to learn. They comprise various habits and abilities that allow children to make social interactions more abundant and deep. They are what helps them find the right people, make friends, and have healthy relationships with their potential partners, colleagues, parents, and relatives in adulthood. The reason you need to start early in developing these skills is that their mind is still in the developmental stage. Whatever they hear, see, or learn today will find a permanent home in their mind. They pick up on the behaviors they see others exhibiting around them. They also take after the language they hear the most in the house, with or without assistance.

This means that everything starts with what kind of environment they are exposed to and the impact that it has on them. If both parents are naturally shy or spend little time with the child, the child has limited interaction and exposure to a healthy social environment. Thus, their vocabulary will be limited, and their habits will be non-concrete and undeveloped.

On the other hand, a child whose parents spend more time in the house with them and make every moment interactive and positive will have very developed habits and social skills. They will be more expressive, curious, and talkative. They will find approaching new people and making friends easier.

They will also be more confident and poised in their nature.

This is the remarkable power of developing good social skills. As a parent, it isn't enough to teach them how to talk or walk, you need to build good habits right from the start. You need to enable them to express themselves and regulate their emotions better. You need to teach them healthy coping mechanisms to build resilience. They need to learn to listen to form better responses. Working with them using the strategies discussed in this book can help parents get started on the right track. Use these to boost their learning and encourage the formation of healthy habits.

Thank you for giving this book a read. I hope you loved reading it as much as I enjoyed writing it. It would make me the happiest person on earth if you would take a moment to leave an honest review. All you have to do is visit the site where you purchased this book: It's that simple! The review doesn't have to be a full-fledged paragraph; a few words will do. Your few words will help others decide if this is what they should be reading as well. Thank you in advance, and best of luck with your parenting adventures. Every moment is a joyous one with a child.

References

Abedon, E. P. (2005, October 3). *Toddler Empathy.* Parents. https://www.parents.com/toddlers-preschoolers/development/behavioral/toddler-empathy/

Bright Horizons Education Team. (2020). *Empathy: A skill for future success.* https://www.brighthorizons.com/family-resources/empathy-a-skill-for-future-success

The Communication Trust. (2011). *Why communication is important.* https://www.thecommunicationtrust.org.uk/media/2147/all_together_now_-_section_2.pdf

Dedic, J. A. (2020, May 7). *14 ways to build your child's social skills from home.* Parents. https://www.parents.com/toddlers-preschoolers/development/social/social-skills-activities-for-kids-to-do-at-home/

Dewar, G. (2019). *The effects of praise: 7 evidence-based tips for praising kids the right way.* Parentingscience.Com. https://www.parentingscience.com/effects-of-praise.html

Diproperzio, L. (2013, July 4). *Social development milestones: Ages 1 to 4.* Parents. https://www.parents.com/toddlers-preschoolers/development/social/social-development-milestones-ages-1-to-4/

Jones, D. E., Greenberg, M., & Crowley, M. (2015). *Early social-emotional functioning and public health: The relationship between kindergarten social competence and future wellness.* American Journal of Public Health, 105(11), 2283–2290. https://doi.org/10.2105/ajph.2015.302630

Kumon. (2016, November). *The importance of children developing good communication skills.* https://www.kumon.co.uk/blog/the-importance-of-children-developing-good-communication-skills/

Lee, K. (2019). *How parents can teach their children good manners around others.* Verywell Family. https://www.verywellfamily.com/teaching-children-manners-620111

Lewis, M. (2015, September 29). *How to teach kids good manners - 6 benefits of proper etiquette.* Moneycrashers.Com. https://www.moneycrashers.com/teaching-kids-good-manners/

Myers, P. (2011, August 17). *The importance of teaching manners to kids.* Child Development Institute. https://childdevelopmentinfo.com/parenting/the-importance-of-teaching-manners-to-kids/#gs.agtnu2

Nair, A. (2018, June 29). *Parallel play: Why is it important for child development?* First Cry. https://parenting.firstcry.com/articles/parallel-play-how-does-it-benefit-your-child/

Newman, S. (2015, October 20). *How to support and nurture your child's passions.* Psychology Today. https://www.psychologytoday.com/us/blog/singletons/201510/how-support-and-nurture-your-childs-passions

Parentingni.org. (2016). *The importance of praise and encouragement.* http://www.parentingni.org/wp-content/uploads/2016/04/Importance-of-Praise-and-Encouragment-2.pdf

PBC Expo. (2020). *Reasons why role playing is important for your child.* https://www.pbcexpo.com.au/blog/reasons-why-role-playing-is-important-for-your-child

Playscheme. (n.d.). *Why is role play important for child development?* https://www.play-scheme.co.uk/why-is-role-play-important-for-child-development/#:~:text=It%20allows%20children%20to%20act

Raising Children Network (Australia). (2017, June 5). *Praise, encouragement and rewards.* https://raisingchildren.net.au/toddlers/connecting-communicating/connecting/praise#:~:text=Praise%20nurtures%20your%20child

Rector, J. (2019, May 9). *The importance of parallel play.* Tinybeans. https://tinybeans.com/articles/the-importance-of-parallel-play/

Resilient Educator. (2013, February 12). *Using empathy to teach social-emotional skills.* https://resilienteducator.com/classroom-resources/role-of-empathy-in-teaching-social-emotional-skills/

Roth, E. (2019, December 7). *Parallel play and toddlers: What it is and why it matters.* Metro Parent. https://www.metroparent.com/daily/parenting/toddlers/parallel-play-and-toddlers-what-it-is-and-why-it-matters/

Segrin, C., & Flora, J. (2000). *Poor social skills are a vulnerability factor in the development of psychosocial problems*. Human Communication Research, 26(3), 489–514. https://doi.org/10.1111/j.1468-2958.2000.tb00766.x

Stephens, K. (2007). *Everyday ways to teach children manners & social skills*. Child Care Exchange. https://www.easternflorida.edu/community-resources/child-development-centers/parent-resource-library/documents/manners-and-social-skills.pdf

Virtual Lab School. (2019). *Social-emotional development: Infants and toddlers*. https://www.virtuallabschool.org/infant-toddler/social-emotional/lesson-2

White, R. (2012, June 11). *Accelerated learning can benefit preschoolers*. Memorise. https://memorise.org/learning/accelerated-learning-benefit-preschoolers

Zero to Three. (2016, February 25). *How to support your child's communication skills*. https://www.zerotothree.org/resources/302-how-to-support-your-child-s-communication-skills

Printed in Great Britain
by Amazon

33586495R00046